INSTRUCTOR'S MANUAL

THE
PLAY'S THE
THING

A WHOLE LANGUAGE
APPROACH TO
LEARNING ENGLISH

VALERIE WHITESON
NAVA HOROVITZ

32 Avenue of the Americas, New York NY 10013-2473, USA

Cambridge University Press is part of the University of Cambridge.

It furthers the University's mission by disseminating knowledge in the pursuit of education, learning and research at the highest international levels of excellence.

www.cambridge.org
Information on this title: www.cambridge.org/9780521657907

First published by St. Martin's Press, Inc.
Reprinted 1999

A catalogue record for this publication is available from the British Library

ISBN 978-0-521-65790-7 Paperback

Contents

Using the Student Textbook

In Act II of *Hamlet* by William Shakespeare, Hamlet says, "The play's the thing to catch the conscience of the King." We believe that the play's the thing to help students learn English and at the same time be introduced to authentic literature in English.

The **Student Textbook** contains 14 units each of which is centered around an excerpt from a play. The reading of the scene from a play provides a springboard for the integration, practice and reinforcement of the four language skills.

Each unit begins with two pre-reading sections. The section called "Introduction" provides students with questions about various aspects of the subject matter of the unit to think about and discuss. The questions require students to explore their knowledge of the subject and to express their opinions. They also work as advance organizers for "About the Play."

Pictures are placed before the play excerpts so students can study the pictures before reading, in order to predict who the characters are, what kind of people they are, the relationships between them, and their roles in the play. The pictures can, in some cases, help the students anticipate what the play is about and what takes place. The students will thus be motivated to read. While reading the excerpt, students will have a mental image of the characters and this will facilitate the reading and comprehension processes. The students can also identify with the characters. After reading the excerpt from the play, the students can then go back to the picture and discuss to what degree their predictions about the play and the characters were accurate.

In the section "About the Play," students are provided first with background information about the playwright, the play, the characters, and, in some cases, important social and historical details.

Thus, before reading the excerpt, the students are already involved and have acquired the tools essential to approaching reading with the appropriate strategies of background knowledge and prediction.

After reading the scene from the play (or listening to a dramatic reading of it on audio cassette) the students are invited to ask questions and the instructor can explain any cultural references the students may not know.

The scene should be read again, either by the instructor or in sections (speeches) by the students in order to better understand the content and, particularly, to get a feel for the language and how it is used.

"Dictionary Work" gives the students an opportunity to look closely at keywords from the scene and to learn their meaning. This section also focuses on the fact that words often have more than one meaning but only one is correct for a particular context. Try to discourage students from using bilingual dictionaries. Students will gain more by learning vocabulary through negotiated meaning. The skills developed here will introduce the students to more general dictionary skills, such as paying attention to spelling, parts of speech, and different meanings.

"Comprehension Questions" encourage the students to return to the text to check for specific information and to take a closer look at details. Short answers, not necessarily complete sentences, where appropriate are acceptable. The focus is on the content and the fluency of the answer rather than the accuracy of the language with which it is expressed. The instructor who wishes to "correct" answers could use this as an opportunity for peer evaluation and ask the students to work in pairs to discuss and make corrections to each other's answers. This section can be assigned for homework with the answers being read and commented on in the following lesson.

"Points to Consider and Discuss" is most suitable for group work (groups of 3 to 5) and an opportunity for the students to improve their oral skills. The students are free to skip topics that do not interest them.

The instructor can allot 15 to 20 minutes for the discussion and circulate in order to answer any questions and to ensure that the rules of polite conversation are observed, that is, listening to other's opinions and turn taking. Explain the importance of speaking only English and remember that there are no correct answers. By working in groups, students also learn the important life skill of collaboration.

"Vocabulary" focuses on vocabulary development using words from the list in "Dictionary Work" to complete sentences and cloze passages. These exercises work well as homework assignments. In some units, a word family chart has been provided so that the students can see the connection between the various parts of speech. This provides the students with an additional strategy for understanding the meaning of words without referring to the dictionary. In the units where there is no chart, the instructor can suggest that the students make one of their own, either with keywords from the scene or words of their choice. The word family chart also provides the different forms of the words required for the language exercises which is an important aid for the less able student.

An additional activity for vocabulary development is "Dictation." The instructor should make up short sentences with the new words for each unit. While the instructor dictates the sentences to the class, one student writes the sentences on the board or on an overhead transparency, while all the other students write in their notebooks. The class reads the sentences on the board and compares them with what they wrote. Suggestions are made to correct errors. The teacher only intervenes if the students cannot help each other.

The instructor can also ask students to write their own sentences using the new words. The students can then ask another student to check their sentences. These activities further recycle the vocabulary for each unit thereby consolidating the learning process.

The focus of "Language" is on developing student awareness of how language is actually used. In most cases, the students' attention is drawn to the differences between written and spoken English. The process of language learning through the acquisition of language chunks has been explained in the introduction to the **Student Textbook**.

The students are encouraged to read aloud phrases and sentences from the scenes in order to improve their pronunciation and intonation. If the students record themselves, they can hear how much better they sound each time.

The "Writing Activities" provide the student with an opportunity to write in a variety of forms: descriptions, lists, letters, dialogues, and recipes. The students can express opinions or use their imaginations, depending on the task at hand. In a course whose focus is on speaking and listening only, this material can be omitted.

Another activity which develops writing skills is to have the students keep a log in which they record their experiences while studying this book. They may like to note opinions or feelings they could not express in class, reactions to what and how they are learning, and any other reflections they may have. Good learners understand not only what they have learned but how they learned it. If you want this to be a dialogue or interactive journal, you can respond regularly or from time to time on what the students have to say.

The section "Prose Passage" in many cases contains a passage thematically related to the play excerpt at the beginning of each unit. Some units include other related activities in this section, such as, reading and filling out a form or following a recipe.

The passages and activities in this section reinforce ideas and vocabulary already stressed in the unit and take the theme of the unit one step further. In some cases, the activities focus on practical applications, such as letter writing, which makes the material relevant to the students' world outside the classroom.

The "Listening Task" section is aimed at developing listening comprehension skills. In order to complete the tasks in this section, the students will listen to the selection provided on the audio cassette. The scripts of the listening comprehension texts appear in this **Instructor's Manual** for the instructor to read to the class if necessary or desired. The texts are of various types including dialogues, lectures, and a poem. The listening tasks require the students to take notes, complete passages with missing words, and mark statements as true or false.

Great trouble has been taken to make the listening comprehension authentic. The production of the listening comprehension passages and the readings of the excerpts will play an important part in developing an awareness in the students to varieties of spoken English.

"Special Assignments" is the last section of each unit. This section provides the students with a variety of challenges suited to different student populations. The students are not expected to do all of these assignments and should be encouraged to choose an assignment that appeals to their special interests and talents and is suited to their ability level. The range of assignments presented in this section means that there is something for every ability level. Creative tasks, such as those included in this section, are motivating.

The completed projects in "Special Assignments" (and in "Writing Activities") can provide contributions to a portfolio. Portfolios are an excellent source for alternative assessment for the instructor and give the students an opportunity to show what they can do in the second/foreign language in a nonthreatening environment. Students will also be given an opportunity to observe their own progress.

Many of the special assignments ask students for information which is most readily available through the Internet. Additional information about the plays and playwrights can be found through this source. If the students want to know more about the cultures and peoples of other countries, they might like to correspond with other students through E-mail. These sources can provide stimulating input which students can put to good use in the classroom discussions and in special activities.

Through studying this book, students will broaden their horizons culturally, emotionally, and linguistically while improving their overall proficiency. Their imaginations will be stimulated and they will develop confidence in their ability to react meaningfully to what they have read and learned.

Answer Key and Tapescripts

As suggested in the section *Using the Book* the focus should be on the content of the answer rather than the accuracy of the language with which it is expressed.

In cases where the answer can be taken directly from the text, those are the words used in the answer provided here. In cases where the answer is implied, the answer is accompanied by the appropriate quotation from the scene as an aid.

The answers to some of the activities are only suggestions and are noted as such. Instructors should be prepared to accept different answers where appropriate.

UNIT 1: HOW DO YOU DO?

Comprehension Questions

1. Yes. "I'm very sorry to have kept you waiting."
2. They shook hands. ". . . and gives him her hand."
3. She asked the way.
4. The professor has lived in the town for thirty years. The pupil has not lived there for long.
5. In Paris or Bordeaux.
6. No. "I don't know them all yet. . . . I have trouble learning them."
7. He is very pleased and says encouraging things.
8. That it takes a little effort and good will and that it will come in time.

Vocabulary

Using the Vocabulary
1. thirsty
2. effort
3. agreeable
4. permit
5. inform
6. progress
7. convince
8. attractive

Cloze Passage
1. bishop
2. agreeable
3. effort
4. inform
5. progress
6. permits
7. convince

Language

1. I beg your pardon.
2. We can't be sure of anything in this world.
3. It's hard.
4. We can't be sure of anything in this world.
5. It will come . . . have patience. You will make real progress.
6. I have a great thirst for knowledge.
7. I'm very sorry to have kept you waiting.
8. It will come . . . have patience. You will make real progress.

Listening Task

Tapescript

pupil: Excuse me.

stranger: Good morning.

pupil: Could you help me, please?

stranger: You look lost. What are you looking for?

pupil: Do you know where the professor lives?

stranger: The professor? Which professor?

pupil: They said he lives somewhere near the church.

stranger: Oh, professor George Lucas?

pupil: Yes, George Lucas. Yes, I think that's his name.

stranger: I can help you, I think. We are now in* First Street.

pupil: Oh yes, I see. First Street.

stranger: Well, go down First Street until the corner.

pupil: OK.

stranger: At the corner, turn right.

pupil: Right at the corner? What's the name of the street?

stranger: I believe it's Main Street.

pupil: Main Street.

stranger: Go down the street for about 200 yards. Pass Second Street.

pupil: Not Second Street.

stranger: That's right. When you see Third Street, turn left.

pupil: Left on Third Street.

stranger: You'll see the church in the distance.

pupil: Oh, yes.

stranger: Walk to Church Circle. Make a left.

pupil: A left on Church Circle?

stranger: Go half way around the circle. You'll see the professor's house across the street from the church.

pupil: What number is it?

stranger: I think it's 327.

pupil: Thank you very much.

stranger: Good luck. I hope you find it. If you don't, ask someone else. Everyone knows the professor around here.

Answers

The professor's name is: George Lucas
The professor's address is: 327 Church Circle

UNIT 2: WHAT DO YOU HAVE TO DO TO BELONG?

Comprehension Questions

1. "... when Mom could finally bring me to the U.S., I was already ten."
2. Clothes. "They'd just stay with themselves and compare how much clothes they all had ..."

---

* This is British usage.

8

3. She thought she had a better chance of being accepted by the white kids. "I figured I had a better chance of getting in with the white kids . . ."
4. She started bleaching her hair and hanging out at the beach.
5. She discovered that she was part of the city. She was lonely and didn't like being alone.

Vocabulary

Using the Vocabulary
1. figure
2. bleach
3. giggling
4. hang out
5. tough
6. breeze
7. lousy

Cloze Passage
1. bleached
2. figure
3. giggle
4. lousy
5. hang out
6. tough

Language

Answering Questions
Suggestions for Grace's answers to the reporter's questions:
About twelve years ago.
Ten years old.
No. It was tough.
No. My mother brought me.
The white kids.
Until my senior year in high school.

Listening Task

Tapescript
Listen to this telephone conversation between Grace and her friend Gloria. While you listen to the conversation write down the following details:
the time; the date; the address; what Grace must bring; who Grace must pick up; his address; his telephone number.
Now listen to the discussion.
[phone rings]
Grace: Hello.
Gloria: Hi, may I speak to Grace?
Grace: Speaking.
Gloria: Oh, hi Grace. This is Gloria. How've you been?
Grace: Fine thanks. How are you?
Gloria: Great. Are you doing anything next Saturday night?
Grace: I don't think so. What's the date?
Gloria: It's the 23 of May.
Grace: That sounds good to me. Is it your birthday?
Gloria: Yes. I'll be 21. Do you know my address?
Grace: No. I've never been to your house.
Gloria: It's 2130 South Street. There's a church on the corner.

Grace: I know where that is. Is there anything I can bring to the party?
Gloria: Can you bring some balloons?
Grace: Sure. Anything else?
Gloria: Will your father lend you his car?
Grace: I guess so. Do you want me to pick someone up?
Gloria: If you don't mind. Do you know my cousin Tony?
Grace: Oh, yes. I'll be happy to give him a ride. Where does he live?
Gloria: He lives at 190 West Ave. in the pink house. His phone number is 723-1211.
Grace: What time do you want us to come?
Gloria: Around eight o'clock.
Grace: OK. Tell Tony I'll pick him up just before eight.
Gloria: That sounds good. I'll see you on Saturday night then.
Grace: Fine. And thanks for thinking of me. Bye.
Gloria: Good-bye.

Answers
the time: around eight o'clock
the date: May 23
the address: 2130 South Street
what Grace must bring: balloons
who Grace must pick up: Gloria's cousin Tony
his address: 190 West Ave.
his phone number: 723-1211

UNIT 3: YOU ARE WHAT YOU EAT

Comprehension Questions

1. The weather is hot. "I thought it'd keep us cool."
2. Because the peaches were warm. She thinks Rachel will like it better.
3. It's supposed to make the nails grow strong.
4. She thinks it's healthier.
5. They like things that taste good.
6. Most of her friends breast feed their babies.
7. Because she is adopting the baby.

Vocabulary

Using the Vocabulary
1. Annie: dessert / recommend / gaining; Betty: brand
2. plain
3. moderate
4. regular
5. comfortable
6. suppose
7. convenient
8. refreshing

Cloze Passage
1. recommended   2. regular / plain

3. brand
4. refreshing
5. plain / regular
6. dessert

7. convenient
8. moderate
9. gain

Language

1. Formal	5. Formal	9. Informal
2. Informal	6. Informal	10. Formal
3. Informal	7. Informal	11. Informal
4. Informal	8. Informal	

2. It is supposed to make their nails grow strong.
3. Yes, but the children will not take it like that.
4. Honey, it does not matter.
5. It does not matter what else you put in front of him, if it is not Sloppy Joe mix, he will not eat it.
6. You are going to have to use formula.
7. They have been around for years and you know they work.

Listening Task

Tapescript

Good evening ladies and gentlemen. I've been invited to speak to you this evening about the kinds of food you should be eating as often as possible. You'll be doing your bodies a favor every time you eat these foods. You can find them in most grocery stores and they are not expensive.

First of all, you should eat as much broccoli as possible even though one of the presidents of the United States said that he doesn't like it. Broccoli fights cancer because it contains vitamin C. Eat it cooked or raw.

Now the next food everyone likes. Don't you like cantaloupe? It also contains vitamin C and something else that is good for you. They give the fruit its color. Cantaloupe helps to prevent heart disease and cancer. It also doesn't contain too many calories, and, of course, it's delicious.

Many people start the day with a glass of orange juice. It's very good for you and it also contains vitamin C. Did you know that a glass of orange juice contains the same amount of calcium as a glass of milk? So make sure that you drink a glass every day.

In some countries they eat lots of dried beans. Yes, they are extremely healthy and don't cost a lot. They are a fantastic source of fiber and they have lots of calcium and protein. If you know how to cook them correctly, they should not upset your stomach. So start eating more beans if you want to be healthier.

We have known for many years that garlic is very healthy. Most people agree that it makes food taste better too. Like cantaloupe it helps to fight heart disease and cancer. Eat as much as you can.

A fairly new food in the Western world is yogurt. Not everybody likes it, but it is very good for you. You should try to eat lowfat yogurt so that you don't gain too much weight. It's a very good source of calcium and a cup of lowfat yogurt is only about 100 calories. You can use it in cooking if you don't like the taste of it.

Another new kind of food that has been used for years in the east is tofu. Some people don't even know what it is. Did you know that women in Japan where they eat a lot of tofu, have lower rates of breast cancer than women in the U.S.A.? There are natural chemicals in tofu and other soy-based products that are very good for you.

A favorite fruit or vegetable is the common tomato. Some people call it a vegetable and others say it is a fruit. Recent research shows that there is something in tomatoes that appears to protect men against prostate cancer.

Another green vegetable that is really healthy for you is watercress. It grows wild in many places and you can find it growing by streams or rivers. It seems to prevent cancer and heavy smokers who eat lots of watercress find that it helps them to overcome the effects of smoking. Most people eat it fresh like lettuce but watercress soup is delicious. If you've never tasted it, try some soon.

Last, but certainly not least, is whole-wheat bread. It is amazing to me to see how many people still eat white bread made from refined flour. Don't they know how healthy the fiber is that you get from whole-wheat flour? If you need more reasons to eat this kind of bread, the fact is that the fiber also helps you to lose weight. It traps some of the fat and helps to carry it out of your body.

I hope that you made a list of these healthy foods. Be sure to eat them as often as possible. I'm off to the market right after this lecture, and do you know what I'm going to buy? . . . I wonder if frozen yogurt will work as well as regular yogurt does?

Answers

1. broccoli
2. cantaloupe
3. orange juice
4. dried beans
5. garlic
6. lowfat yogurt
7. tofu
8. tomatoes
9. watercress
10. whole-wheat bread

UNIT 4: ARE WE READY FOR THE FUTURE?

Comprehension Questions

1. Because our time will be valuable and it will not make sense to spend it taking care of things.
2. A radio, any machine or appliance.
3. Paper cups, paper plates, and paper towels.
4. We will make a call on the telephone and a new one will be delivered.
5. Yes. Because they have no real values and are busy with unimportant things. "I think most people are. . . . I mean that we are base, and that we spend our lives with small things."
6. No, she doesn't. "You are not base."

Vocabulary

Using the Vocabulary

1. offended
2. feasible
3. value
4. mend (repair)
5. appliance
6. decent
7. breaks down / repair (mend)
8. hollow

Language

Adjectives
valuable painting
hollow promise
offensive comment
decent person
base act
feasible suggestion

2. valuable painting
3. offensive comment
4. decent person
5. base act
6. feasible suggestion

2. b. Will you go with me to buy the bike?
3. a. OK, I'll go with you.
4. a. Where will you get the money?
5. b. I'll take it.
6. a. I won't be able to. It's too far.

Prose Passage

Many books have been written about the future. One of the most famous is *Future Shock* by Alvin Toffler, written in 1970. This is what Toffler thinks will happen to the family in the future. (The three sentences left out of the passage are indicated in bold type.)

> In the future, there will be fewer people in the family. In the old days, families had many children. (1) **It was not unusual to have ten or more children in a family.** Families were made up of parents, grandparents, children, uncles and aunts, and cousins. This kind of family was very good because people took care of each other.
>
> Today, this kind of family does not work so well. It is difficult and expensive to move a large family. In order to get a job today, workers must be ready to move to places where jobs can be found. (2) **Workers may have to move many times during their lives.** In the Western world today, most families are small. They are made up of parents and very few children.
>
> In the future, it may be better for couples to delay having a family while they are working. So a typical family of the future will be only a husband and wife. According to Margaret Mead, the famous anthropologist, some families will be "chosen" to have children. Others will work and not have any children. Many families will wait until they retire from their jobs before they have children. (3) **In the future, people will probably live much longer lives.** New developments in science will make it possible for people to have children when they are old.

Listening Task

Tapescript
Listen to this speech given by Ngan Pham. While you listen, read the text of Ngan's talk. Try to fill in the missing words.

Hi, I'm Ngan Pham from the O. B. Whaley Elementary school in San Jose, California. I'm ten years old and I'll be talking to you (1) **about** teachers of the twenty-first century. Being a teacher in the twenty-first century will (2) **be** a lot different from now. It (3) **will** be easier for teachers and students.

The classroom will (4) **change** because everyone will get a computer. The computer hard drive will have (5) **your** work instead of (6) **putting** it into your desk. The computer will also have your books. If you (7) **can't** read, the computer will read to you (8) **so** you can follow along and learn to read.

(9) **Everything** will be in the computer, including your reference books, text books, math books, and (10) **other** books. With the computer you will not have a messy (11) **desk** to clean up. Learning will be easier for students (12) **because** of (13) **a** thinking cap. The thinking cap has a computer chip inside to help students remember (14) **what** they are reading about.

Teachers in the twenty-first century will (15) **also** need a lot (16) **of** training. They will go to school and learn things to teach (17) **their** students. They will learn many things (18) **like** we do. Teachers will need lots of training on computers because they have to plan (19) **programs** for the students. The teachers will also have to set up (20) **the** programs for the students so that the students will be (21) **able** to read along (22) **with** the computer.

Many times students get sick and can't come to school. (23) **But** in the future, when students get sick and can't (24) **go** to school, they'll take their computers home and the computers will show (25) **them** what the teacher said. If there is (26) **homework**, the teacher will fax it to them.

In conclusion, (27) **I** think that teaching will be easier (28) **and** the best job in the twenty-first century.

UNIT 5: WHAT IS THIS ALL ABOUT?

Comprehension Questions

1. An envelope.
2. Twelve matches.
3. No. "Nothing on it. Not a word."
4. No. "No one."
5. He takes them out of his pocket.
6. A revolver.
7. Yes. "Well, they'll come in handy. . . . Yes, I could do with them."
8. They plan to use them to light the kettle.
9. They argue about whether you say "light the kettle" or "light the gas."
10. No.

Vocabulary

1. dozen / run out	5. reasonable
2. sealed	6. kettle
3. senior partner	7. revolver
4. come in handy	8. partner

1. match	5. anyone / replace
2. catch	6. towards
3. menacing	7. pillow
4. examine	8. stared

Language

1. . . . much too fond of the bottle. = He drinks too much.
2. . . . from the cradle to the grave. = From birth to death.
3. . . . respect for the bench. = Respect for the judge and what he represents.
4. The palace should not look down on the cottage. = The rich should not look down on the poor.
5. One sees the mud, and one the stars. = One sees something bad (negative), the other something good (positive); one is an optimist, the other a pessimist.
6. I never promised you a rose garden. = I never said that everything would be pleasant.
7. . . . a bowl of cherries = Good, pleasant, colorful; see above.

Language Chunks

1. I don't know. / They'll come in handy.
2. Who me? / What is it? / Where did it come from?
3. I don't know.
4. Go on.
5. What is it?
6. What is it?
7. I don't know.
8. Who me?

Listening Task

Tapescript*

Harold Pinter was born at Hackney, East London, in England. He was born in 1930 on October 10. His father was a tailor and his mother stayed at home to take care of him. Pinter believes that his father's family came to England from Hungary. There are people in Hungary with the name of Pinter. Before the family moved to Hungary, they probably lived in Spain or Portugal. The family think** the name was Pinto, da Pinto, or da Pinta. Many Jews who were expelled from Spain and Portugal moved to other places in Europe like Hungary.

Pinter says: "I lived in a brick house near Clapton Pond. There were a few ducks on the pond. It was a working-class area. There was a soap factory with a terrible smell. There were railway yards and lots of shops.

"My mother was a marvelous cook and still is. My father worked terribly hard. He worked a twelve-hour day, making clothes in his shop."

When the Second World War began, Harold Pinter was sent to live in a castle in Cornwall. This is what he says about it: "I went to a castle in Cornwall with twenty-four other boys. It had marvelous grounds. And it was on the sea. It looked out on the English channel." He was not happy there and after a year, he went back to London. Later he was sent away again but his mother went with him.

In 1944, he saw his first flying bomb. He was in the street and he saw it come over. Although their house was never bombed, they had to leave it often to go to a shelter. Pinter says that every time he had to leave the house, he took his cricket bat with him.

After the war, Pinter studied at Hackney Downs Grammar School. It was a boys' school and there were about six hundred boys. He didn't like most of his teachers except for his

---

* Harold Pinter. Interview in *The New Yorker*, February 25, 1967.
** This is British usage.

15

English master, Joseph Brearley. Pinter says: "He's a very brilliant man. He's a great fellow. He was obsessed with the theater. I played Macbeth when I was sixteen, and he directed me, and then he directed me when I played Romeo. I went in for football and cricket at school and I was always chosen to run. My main ability was sprinting. I set a new school record—a hundred yards in ten point two but it's been broken since. The only universities I was thinking about were Oxford and Cambridge. But you had to know Latin, and I didn't know Latin. . . ."

Answers

1. True	8. False	15. True
2. True	9. True	16. True
3. True	10. True	17. False
4. False	11. False	18. False
5. True	12. False	19. False
6. True	13. True	20. False
7. True	14. False	

UNIT 6: FATHERS AND DAUGHTERS

Comprehension Questions

1. Business usually.
2. He wonders if she will study penmanship or word processing and how he will pay for her graduate school.
3. No, he doesn't ask her. Because she starts to talk about the clouds.
4. She sees the head of Walter Cronkite in a vase, two big elbows, and two elephant trunks dancing. He also sees something that looks like Walter Cronkite in a vase.
5. When Paul points out the moving cloud that looks like a whale on a thimble, Lisa sees it too.

Vocabulary

1. erupt	6. thimble
2. whale	7. stomach
3. actually	8. word processing
4. business	9. psychiatrist
5. graduate	10. penmanship

Listening Task

Tapescript

Children who grow up in the same family don't grow up in the same world if they are boys and girls. People don't usually speak to girls the same way that they speak to boys. People also expect boys to speak differently from girls. One of the main reasons for this is that girls generally learn how to speak by copying their mothers and boys learn from their fathers. And men and women don't use language the same way.

In most countries, boys usually play with boys and girls play with girls. Some of the things they do are the same, but often their favorite games are different. And the way they use language in these games is different too.

Boys usually play outside. Often there is a leader who tells the other boys what to do and how to do it. The leader doesn't like to get advice from others and when he does, he doesn't take the advice. Boys also like to tell jokes and stories. One boy likes to tell better stories and jokes than the other boys. Boys' games always have winners and losers. They also like to boast and say that they are the strongest or the best.

Girls are different. They like to play in small groups or pairs. The most important person in a girl's social life is her best friend. When girls play such games as jump rope or hopscotch, everyone gets a turn. Girls love to play house and there are no winners and losers. Some girls are better than others but they never boast about it. A girl never says, "I'm the best."

Girls never give orders. They say something like, "How about doing that?" or "Let's do that." Boys are much more direct. They say, "Get outta here" or "Gimme that." Girls try not to be bossy. They try to be kind to each other. Their main concern is to be liked and popular with the other girls. Most of the time girls sit together and talk.

Answers

1. False	5. True	9. False
2. True	6. False	10. True
3. True	7. True	11. True
4. False	8. True	12. True

UNIT 7: WILL YOU MARRY ME?

Comprehension Questions

1. At school.
2. Her boyfriend was waiting for her.
3. He carried her books.
4. Yes. "Glad I came? / You know I am."
5. She likes winter.
6. He likes winter because it gets dark early and gives him more time to kiss her.
7. No, she doesn't mind.
8. Nearly eighteen.
9. Yes. They love each other.
10. She won't mind. "She'll probably laugh. . . . she isn't prejudiced against color."
11. They plan to marry on his next leave.
12. They'll save some money.

Vocabulary

1. prejudiced	4. resist
2. kidding	5. probably
3. adore	6. leave

Language

Asking Questions

The answers to this exercise are the ones from the text as instructed. Some suggestions for the second task have also been given. These are suggestions only.

2. Glad I came? / Are you listening to me?
3. Afraid someone'll see us? / Don't you think it's dangerous?

4. Will you marry me? / Can we go steady?
5. How old are you? / Are you eighteen yet?
6. How do you know? / Why do you love me?
7. What will your mother say? / How will your friend react?
8. Doesn't she care who her daughter marries? / Do you want to ask your sister for her advice?
9. You're not worried about it, are you? / Do you think your brother will like it?
10. When shall we get married? / Will you wait for six months?

Language Chunks
2. I said so, didn't I?
3. Not yet. / I said so, didn't I? / You know I am.
4. I don't care. / Not really.
5. Not really. / Say that again.
6. Not really. / You know I am. / Not yet.

Listening Task

Tapescript

Seaman's Ditty
Gary Snyder

I'm wondering where you are now
Married or mad or free;
Wherever you are you're likely glad,
But memory troubles (1) **me**.

We could've had us children
We could have had a (2) **home**—
But you thought not, and I (3) **thought** not,
And these nine years we roam.

Today I worked in the deep dark tanks,
And climbed out to watch the (4) **sea**;
Gulls and salty waves pass by,
And mountains of Araby.

I've traveled the lonely oceans
And wandered the (5) **lonely** towns.
I've learned a (6) **lot** and lost a lot,
And proved the world was (7) **round**.

Now if we'd stayed together,
There's much we'd never've known—
But dreary books and (8) **dreary** lands
Weigh on (9) **me** like a (10) **stone**.

UNIT 8: WILL YOU HELP ME FIND A JOB?

Comprehension Questions

1. First she uses only her first name afterwards she also uses her family name.
2. When they were children. "A childhood friend of my wife's. . . . Yes, we knew each other in earlier days."
3. Head of the bank.
4. From their local newspaper.
5. She has quite a bit of experience.

Vocabulary

1. sensible / widow
2. experiences / childhood
3. presume / absolutely
4. imagine / mad

Language

The answers given here are just suggestions. You can accept any suitable answer given by the students.

2. I presume she did.
3. I hope he will.
4. I'm sure he is.
5. Yes he does.
6. I suppose they are.

7. Yes I will.
8. I'm certain you are.
9. I think I have.
10. I presume you were.

Listening Task

Tapescript

Good morning students.

Now that you've finished your course, I want to give you some advice about how to interview for a job. Of course, this will depend on where you live to a certain extent. In the U.S.A. you have to be less modest than in many other countries. But the advice I'm going to give you will be good anywhere you are.

Don't arrive too early for your interview. There was a man who arrived two hours early for a job at our college. The office staff were* disturbed by him as he kept asking them questions about the job. Do I need to tell you that he didn't get the job? So arrive on time—that means about ten minutes or so before your appointment.

Try to find out how people dress in the place where you want to work before you go for your interview. In most places, people dress smartly but simply. If you come to your interview wearing your most elegant clothes, I don't think you'll get the job. In many companies in the U.S.A. on Fridays workers dress more casually. I don't know why that's happened.

Before you leave for the interview, think about what you need to take with you. I always take copies of my diplomas and certificates with me in case they need them. It's true that you can always send them later, but I've found that having them with me works much better. It's good to be able to give them the copies if they ask to see them.

---

* This is British usage.

I also take copies of references with me to the interviews. This way, if they ask about my experience, I can give them copies of references without problems. I know you can send them later, but I believe that it's better to take them along with you.

Some people say you should act yourself at an interview. They say, "What you see is what you get." I must confess that I think they're wrong. You have to be on your best behavior when you go for an interview. My advice is to be courteous and cheerful.

Some of my students speak very quietly. They speak so quietly that I tell them, "If they can't hear you, they won't hire you!" Don't speak too loudly either. Try to match the way your interviewer speaks. It's also not a good idea to answer all questions with yes or no. Don't talk too much, yes, but do give full answers to their questions.

One of the most difficult things to do at an interview is to sell yourself while at the same time trying to remain modest. Probably the best advice I can give you is to tell you to tell the truth. When I got my last job as a teacher they asked me: "Why should we hire you?" I told them that I could teach any course in the English department. I think they were impressed. So don't oversell yourself but don't be shy either.

If they offer you the job and tell you the salary and conditions, don't comment. That's the job they're offering you. If the conditions and salary don't suit you, don't accept the job. If you don't like something but still want the job, try to change things later. It's not a good idea to do it at your first interview.

I'm sure there are other things I ought to tell you but I can't think of anything else. I want to thank you all for studying with us. Good luck and do stay in touch.

Answers

The speaker makes the following statements:
2. Make sure that you arrive on time.
3. Do dress smartly but simply.
5. Do bring all your diplomas and/or certificates showing qualifications.
7. If they ask for references, you can send them later.
8. Do bring references showing previous experience.
9. Try to be courteous and cheerful.
11. Don't talk too much or too loudly.
15. Don't criticize the work conditions or the salary.

UNIT 9: NATURE OR NURTURE

Comprehension Questions

1. That the situation will change or get better as the person grows up.
2. "It" is a gun.
3. She thinks he'll go back to school or get a job.
4. She doesn't agree. She thinks he'll go to jail. "I hope they put him away. . . . I'd turn him in myself . . ."
5. He stole two rings and other valuable things.
6. She means that although they wear the same size pants, they have a different character. They are different people.

Vocabulary

1. dress up
2. manicure
3. loose
4. tore

5. get even	8. boards
6. valuable	9. lay
7. assault	10. armed

Language

Spoken vs. Written Language

2. This is just a stage Ricky is going through.
3. I would report him to the police myself if I knew where he was.
4. That is just the same size. That does not mean you are the same person.
5. We look out at the world and see the same thing: It is not fair.
6. And the only difference between us is that Ricky is out there trying to get even.

Prose Passage

1. intelligence
2. they do not measure artistic, musical, social, or athletic abilities / they do not measure motivation
3. that they are intelligent
4. they are motivated
5. have a low I.Q. / were not born in the right family or the right place.

Listening Task

Tapescript

Question: If you had a student in your school who had been stealing, what would you do about it? How/what would you advise the pupil (1) **or parents**?

Susan Sofer: I (2) **would invite** the whole family for a meeting. I'd call them (3) **all in** and have them talk about what's (4) **going on** in their lives. Whether this is the first time (5) **or if** something is going on in the family that (6) **is different**. And depending on their answer, I would recommend that they (7) **follow up** with more intensive counseling or therapy (8) **with a** private therapist who could discuss what is going on . . . what (9) **brought it on**. I'd also want to know if this is, this is a pattern (10) **or if it's** something new in this child's life. But, (11) **in general**, I would recommend that (12) **the family** make an effort to go and seek ongoing family therapy or individual (13) **therapy**.

Question: So you think it's a symptom (14) **rather than** somebody stealing just because they want something?

Susan Sofer: It can be (15) **a symptom** or it can also be a part of teenage rebellion or (16) **getting attention**. In that case the family needs to (17) **deal with** the fact that the child has chosen to do this as (18) **his or her** rebellion.

UNIT 10: DO YOU BELIEVE IN LUCK?

Comprehension Questions

1. August.
2. August.
3. Because he thinks a horoscope is for predicting the future and not for examining the past.

21

4. Kate. To find out if November 25 was Larry's favorable day.
5. Keller believes in them but Jim doesn't. "Well, was that his favorable day? . . . He's just completely out of his mind . . ."
6. Jim thinks Frank is an idiot, "Jim looking at him as though at an idiot." Jim thinks he's crazy, "He's just completely out of his mind . . ."
7. He believes in everything.
8. That he doesn't believe in anything.

Vocabulary

Predicting the Future

1. horoscopes	4. assume
2. according	5. reported
3. practically	6. miss

Language

2. That is for the future, isn't it?
3. Well, what I am doing is this, you see.
4. Am I right that Larry was reported missing on November 25?
5. Oh, did Kate ask you to make a horoscope?
6. What is a favorable day? / What does a favorable day mean?
7. Well, was November 25 his favorable day?
8. He is completely out of his mind.

Prose Passage

This cloze passage may be difficult for some of the less able students. Therefore, the instructor can provide the answer key (scrambled, of course) as a bank of words to be filled in if desired. The activity can be made more difficult than a simple fill-in exercise by adding some distractors. This would still be easier for some students than a cloze passage.

As an alternative for less able students, the passage could be divided into sections. The students could work on a small section only and then share and exchange words with a partner or other members of a group.

1. what	11. like	21. up
2. if	12. that	22. end
3. few	13. get	23. something
4. very	14. but	24. the
5. in	15. right	25. between
6. it	16. and	26. is
7. than	17. want	27. look
8. carpet	18. have	28. not
9. do	19. one	29. yourself
10. as	20. scream	30. new

Listening Task

Tapescript

The action in *All My Sons* takes place in the back yard of the Keller home near Columbus,

Ohio. The time of the play is about three years after the end of World War II. There are four people in the Keller family: Joe, Kate, Larry, and Chris. Joe Keller is the head of the family.

The Kellers are typical of an average American family. Their son, Larry, has been missing since the war. He was in the Air Force during the war.

Joe, the father, has not had much formal education, but he has worked hard all his life to build a successful business. His family's comfort and social position depend on this business. During the war, Joe Keller's business sold faulty engine parts to the Air Force. The worst part about this is that they knew the parts were no good. Joe Keller also betrayed his best friend and partner, Herbert Deever. Joe Keller did not admit that he, too, was responsible for selling defective parts to the Air Force. Then Joe Keller lied about it in court. He allowed Deever to take the blame. Deever was ruined by being sent to jail. He brought great shame to his family.

Kate Keller, Joe's wife, wants to forget Joe's crimes. She is afraid that they might have some connection to Larry's death. Mrs. Keller looks for all sorts of signs to prove to her family that Larry is still alive. She is even ready to sacrifice the happiness of her second son, Chris. Chris is in love with Anne who was Larry's girlfriend. His mother does not want Chris to marry her. Anne also happens to be Herbert Deever's daughter.

With the help of these characters and others in the play, such as the neighbors, Arthur Miller presents us with many social and moral conflicts, like family loyalty, crime and punishment, and parent-children relationships.

Answers

1. True	6. True	11. False
2. False	7. True	12. False
3. False	8. False	13. True
4. True	9. True	14. False
5. False	10. True	15. True

UNIT 11: JOB SATISFACTION

Comprehension Questions

1. They go off to a strange place or spend the time shut up at home.
2. When they come back, they are more depressed because they have to start all over again.
3. He's fed up with the job. He feels that he is like a parrot—repeating himself endlessly.
4. He really loved his job and was inspired by the students.
5. He was enthusiastic as he was going to shape people's lives. He would be better than other teachers.
6. He compares teachers to actors who have learned a part.

Vocabulary

1. naive	5. paranoid	9. enthusiastic
2. depressed	6. inspired	10. questionable
3. responsible	7. bitter	11. inevitable
4. sheer	8. nasty	

Listening Task

Tapescript

Audience: How did you learn to become a stage manager?

Hatch: I studied Theater as an undergraduate at my university. And now I learn on the job all the time.

Audience: Are there any books to help you?

Hatch: Oh, yes. This book is my bible. All the stage managers I know use this book to help them with their jobs.

Audience: Did you work in the theater before you got this job?

Hatch: I acted and worked with scenery and sound and costumes. I also worked as an electrician in the theater.

Audience: What does an assistant stage director actually do?

Hatch: You could say that the assistant stage manager acts as the liaison between the director and the actors. I have a list of all the actors with their phone numbers and addresses. I make sure that they're in the right place at the right time. During rehearsals I'm in charge of the props and costumes too. In *Coriolanus*, the play we're doing now, I have to be sure that the actors are carrying the right weapons. If an actor has a headache or a cold, I'm the person with the tissues and the aspirins. I have so much responsibility with this play *Coriolanus* that I need an assistant.

Audience: What does the stage manager do?

Hatch: After all the rehearsals and when the show actually starts, many directors leave. Then the stage manager takes over the responsibility for the play. They have to know everything about the production.

Audience: How do you remember everything?

Hatch: We have computers with us and we make notes of any changes. Before the show goes on, we work very hard.

Audience: I've noticed that sometimes actors change their costumes so quickly it seems impossible. How do they do that?

Hatch: I'll let you into* a secret. They wear one costume on top of another. That way they can take off the top costume and be ready in seconds.

Audience: What is that hanging around your neck?

Hatch: It's one of the most important tools of the trade. It's a stopwatch. In this business, time and timing is very important.

Audience: What is the biggest challenge for you in a show?

Hatch: Children and animals. We all take extra care when we have them in a show. You never know what they're going to do next. They have special handlers to take care of them.

Audience: What are your plans for the future?

Hatch: I found out that I'm not a very good actor and I am good as a stage manager. In fact, what I really want is to be a director.

Audience: What happens when something goes wrong during a performance?

Hatch: We know that the show must go on. We find a way. If one of the actors gets sick or falls and hurts themselves, the understudy takes over. Sometimes the stage manager has to explain what happened to the audience and ask them to be patient and understanding. Do you have any more questions for me? . . . Thank you for coming to this discussion. Enjoy the play.

---

* This is British usage.

Answers

1. False. He did go to college.
2. False. He does learn part of the job from a book.
3. True.
4. False. He is not a good actor.
5. True.
6. True.
7. False. They carry weapons.
8. False. When the show starts, many directors leave.
9. True.
10. True.
11. False. Computers are useful.
12. True.
13. False. They can cause some problems.
14. True.
15. True.
16. False. He loves his job.
17. False. It is a difficult job.
18. True.

UNIT 12: WHICH IS MORE IMPORTANT—THE PAST, PRESENT, OR FUTURE?

Comprehension Questions

1. Papa Willie Boy did.
2. He is their father.
3. No, she doesn't. / No.
4. He wants to buy land and farm it.
5. It reminds her of the past of her family.
6. Yes, he believes that his father would have understood.
7. She polished it with her blood.
8. She says that they are fools who kill and steal.

Vocabulary

1. sentimental
2. thieves
3. polish
4. pray
5. suppose
6. carvings
7. rot
8. seeds
9. crop

Language

2. You can not do anything with that piano in the house.
3. That is something else.
4. I would have to say that Berniece uses the piano.
5. That is all right.
6. You do not have anything that is working for you.

7. You are not taking that piano out of my house.
8. You always talk about your father; however, you have never stopped to consider what his foolishness cost your mother.
9. What did it ever lead to?
10. It never stops.

Prose Passage

1. Nettie writes that "the Egyptians who built the pyramids and enslaved the Israelites were colored. . . ."
2. They sold them because they loved money more than their brothers and sisters.
3. They got to America in ships.
4. They were slaves who had to work.
5. According to Nettie, the pictures in the Bible are wrong because, although they depict white people, the words in the Bible describe people who were not white. The Ethiopians like "Jesus Christ had hair like lamb's wool."
6. Jesus Christ was not white and his hair was very curly.

UNIT 13: ARRANGING A MARRIAGE

Comprehension Questions

1. No, Jack is not on her list. She had never heard of him before.
2. She's glad that he smokes and she believes that every man needs an occupation.
3. She thinks it's a good age to marry.
4. She is glad to hear it.
5. She thinks that it has no effect at all.
6. He says he has between seven and eight thousand pounds a year.
7. Owning land is not a good investment.
8. She is an unspoiled, simple young woman.
9. Jack does not know who his parents were as he was abandoned at birth.
10. See question 9.
11. Jack was found in a hand-bag in the cloak-room in Victoria Station by Mr. Thomas Cardew.
12. She advises him to find some relatives and one parent, at least.

Vocabulary

1. single
2. respectfully
3. idle
4. exotic
5. investments
6. tampered
7. radical
8. reside
9. advanced
10. presume
11. aristocracy
12. charitable
13. handle
14. particular
15. contempt

Language

4. I don't agree with anything that affects people who know nothing.
10. Where did Mr. Cardew find this ordinary hand-bag?
12. It's true that I would do everything to make Gwendolen happy.

UNIT 14: THE GREATEST PERSON WHO EVER LIVED

Comprehension Questions

Suggested answers:
1. Hally: That makes two of us.
   Hally: And anyway who are you to talk?
   Sam: No, Hally.
   Etc.
2. Sam: Anyway, I still don't believe it.
   Hally: God, you're impossible. I showed it to you in black and white.
   Sam: Doesn't mean I got to believe it.
   Etc.
3. Hally: And anyway who are you to talk?
   Hally: God, you're impossible.
   Hally: It's the likes of you that kept the Inquisition in business.
   Etc.
4. Sam wants to remind Hally that he has not read much Shakespeare either.
5. Halley chooses Tolstoy and Sam chooses Alexander Fleming.
6. Sam's choice shows that Hally's attempts to educate him have been successful.

Vocabulary

1. moldy
2. intellectual
3. digested
4. based
5. benefit
6. geniuses
7. reserve
8. struggle

Answer Key: Grammar Focus

UNIT 1

Present Simple Tense / Present Continuous (Progressive) Tense

1. studies
2. am studying
3. eat / leave

4. is raining / is running
5. plays / is playing

1./e. I study French and Arabic with very good teachers.
2./c. I am studying French for an important exam.
3./f. She does the laundry on Mondays.
4./i. She's taking an art course at the university.
5./j. He uses a computer at work.
6./h. He's using a pencil to draw that picture.
7./b. We go there by bus.
8./g. We are going there by bus today.
9./d. I work for my mother in her boutique.
10./a. I'm working for my mother until I start college.

Question Forms

1. You like baseball, don't you? / You like baseball?
2. Is this party fun?
3. Do you know everyone here?
4. You have eaten something, haven't you?
5. Would you like a lift home?
6. Is Sharon a wonderful hostess?
7. Are people leaving already?
8. You will be coming to Ben's party next week, won't you?

UNIT 2

Past Tense

1./h. We played football last winter.
2./f. She walks to school when her bike is broken.
3./a. The teacher was ill so she didn't come for a week.
4./b. Man first walked on the moon in 1969.
5./c. She plays the piano at school social events.
6./d. They watched TV until midnight last night.
7./e. I visited him a week ago.
8./g. He crashed his car when he ran a red light.
Two of the sentences are in the present simple tense. Six are in the past simple tense.

1. was / arrived
2. took
3. had

4. made / were
5. bought / began
6. forgot

UNIT 3

Past Tense "Used To" and "Used"

1. used
2. am used to
3. used to
4. use / are used to
5. used to
6. got used to
7. are used to
8. uses

Present Perfect Tense

1. has seen
2. have eaten
3. have lived
4. has written
5. have stayed
6. has broken
7. has been
8. have prepared

UNIT 4

Future Tense

1. will spend
2. will visit
3. will consist
4. will be eaten
5. will be done
6. will have
7. will be destroyed
8. will happen

UNIT 6

More on the Future Tense

1. will be
2. will be eating
3. will be speaking
4. will finish
5. will build

UNIT 7

Negatives

1. I couldn't find it.
2. She won't look again.
3. They weren't there.
4. You mustn't forget next time.
5. You shouldn't expect miracles.

UNIT 8

Modals

1. possible

2. possible / permitted

29

3. advisable
4. necessary
5. possible
6. possible

7. permitted
8. polite request
9. certainty
10. advice

1. should
2. must
3. must
4. can
5. might

6. can / should
7. could
8. can / may
9. must
10. Would

Adjectives

1. little
2. clever
3. childhood
4. impossible
5. lucky

UNIT 9

Language Chunks

She'll grow out of this.
She just needs time.
It's just something she's going through.
You don't mean that.

UNIT 10

Passive Form

1. is broken
2. has been delivered
3. is being ruined
4. was written

5. had been served
6. were killed
7. was being cleaned
8. was filmed

1./c. I won't clean that room again. It was cleaned yesterday.
2./d. That was a very serious accident. It was caused by a drunk driver.
3./a. I won't speak to her again. She was very rude at the party.
4./b. I baked two cakes yesterday. They have both been eaten.
5./f. Children love to play with toys. It does not matter if they are old and broken.
6./e. He has been arrested. He's being questioned by the police.
7./h. Football can be dangerous. I broke my leg twice playing it.
8./g. A new swimming pool is being built in this area. I hope it has been planned for safety.
Three of the sentences above are phrased in the active voice. Five use the passive.

UNIT 11

Pronouns

1. We	6. my
2. I	7. himself
3. I	8. They
4. my	9. we
5. he	10. ourselves

1. mine, he / she, my, I, it, him / her, he / she, it
2. My, they, their, I, them, their
3. my, I, I, I, them

UNIT 12

Synonyms and Antonyms

1. found / lost	6. argument
2. opinion / judgment	7. hate / despise
3. value / worth	8. sabbatical / year's vacation
4. pleased / glad	9. polished / rubbed
5. loves	

UNIT 13

Articles

1. an / the	5. an
2. the / the	6. a / a
3. the / the / the	7. a / the
4. a / an / a / the	8. the

UNIT 14

Ellipsis

1. benefited all mankind (line 6)
2. where we come from and what it all means (line 23)
3. man of magnitude (line 31)
4. play by Shakespeare (line 46)
5. plays by Shakespeare (line 48)
6. play by Shakespeare (line 49)
7. of magnitude (line 64)
8. who don't understand Freud (line 115)

Lightning Source UK Ltd.
Milton Keynes UK
UKOW07f0626121214

243048UK00001B/61/P